Dick Whittington
AND
His Cat

retold by MARGARET HODGES

illustrated by MÉLISANDE POTTER

HOLIDAY HOUSE / *New York*

Retold from *The History of Sir Rich[ard] Whittington Thrice Lord-Mayor of London*
Printed and Sold at the Printing-Office in Bow-Church-Yard   n. d.
in the Elizabeth Nesbitt Room Chapbook Collection,
Information Sciences Library, University of Pittsburgh

Text copyright © 2006 by Margaret Hodges
Illustrations copyright © 2006 by Mélisande Potter
All Rights Reserved
Printed in the United States of America
The text typeface is Olduvai Regular.
The illustrations were rendered in inks and gouache on Strathmore paper.
www.holidayhouse.com
First Edition
1 3 5 7 9 10 8 6 4 2

Library of Congress Cataloging-in-Publication Data
Hodges, Margaret, 1911–2005
Dick Whittington and his cat / retold by Margaret Hodges ; illustrated by Mélisande Potter.— 1st ed.
p. cm.
Summary: Retells the legend of the poor boy in medieval England who trades his beloved cat
for a fortune in gold and jewels and eventually becomes Lord Mayor of London.
ISBN-10: 0-8234-1987-8 (hardcover)
ISBN-13: 978-0-8234-1987-6 (hardcover)
1. Whittington, Richard, d. 1423—Legends—Juvenile literature.
[1. Whittington, Richard, d. 1423—Legends. 2. Folklore—England.] I. Whittington and his cat.
II. Potter, Mélisande, ill. III. Whittington and his cat. English. IV. Title.
PZ8.1.H69Dic 2006
398.2'0942'04529752—dc22
[E]
2005046222

ON A LONG-AGO DAY, Dick Whittington sat on a stone by an English c
Dick's father and mother had died, and he was all alone in the world. Tim
in his village. No one could give him more than a few scrapings of porri
bread. A signpost pointed to London—20 miles. Hungry and cold, he cl
tried not to cry.

Dick Whittington AND His Cat

retold by MARGARET HODGES

illustrated by MÉLISANDE POTTER

HOLIDAY HOUSE / New York

To the long-ago children who loved the chapbooks
M. H.

To Pia and Isabel,
and felines Bella, Aurora, Potpourri, Boots, and Henry
M. P.

Retold from *The History of Sir Rich[ard] Whittington Thrice Lord-Mayor of London*
Printed and Sold at the Printing-Office in Bow-Church-Yard   n. d.
in the Elizabeth Nesbitt Room Chapbook Collection,
Information Sciences Library, University of Pittsburgh

Text copyright © 2006 by Margaret Hodges
Illustrations copyright © 2006 by Mélisande Potter
All Rights Reserved
Printed in the United States of America
The text typeface is Olduvai Regular.
The illustrations were rendered in inks and gouache on Strathmore paper.
www.holidayhouse.com
First Edition
1 3 5 7 9 10 8 6 4 2

Library of Congress Cataloging-in-Publication Data
Hodges, Margaret, 1911–2005
Dick Whittington and his cat / retold by Margaret Hodges ; illustrated by Mélisande Potter.— 1st ed.
p. cm.
Summary: Retells the legend of the poor boy in medieval England who trades his beloved cat
for a fortune in gold and jewels and eventually becomes Lord Mayor of London.
ISBN-10: 0-8234-1987-8 (hardcover)
ISBN-13: 978-0-8234-1987-6 (hardcover)
1. Whittington, Richard, d. 1423—Legends—Juvenile literature.
[1. Whittington, Richard, d. 1423—Legends. 2. Folklore—England.] I. Whittington and his cat.
II. Potter, Mélisande, ill. III. Whittington and his cat. English. IV. Title.
PZ8.1.H69Dic 2006
398.2'*0942'04529752—dc22
[E]
2005046222

ON A LONG-AGO DAY, Dick Whittington sat on a stone by an English country road. Dick's father and mother had died, and he was all alone in the world. Times were hard in his village. No one could give him more than a few scrapings of porridge or a crust of bread. A signpost pointed to London—20 miles. Hungry and cold, he closed his eyes and tried not to cry.

Then he heard the hooves of a farm horse, *clop, clop, clop*; and a man driving a load of hay called, "What's the matter, boy? Want a ride to London?"

"Oh yes, sir," said Dick, and he climbed up beside the driver.

"What will you do in London?" asked the driver.

"I'll find work," Dick answered. "All the people in London are rich."

"And the streets are paved with gold?" said the driver, laughing at him.

But when Dick finally jumped down from the wagon onto a London street, it was not paved with gold, and trash lay strewn about. Dick saw many poor, old, and homeless people. No one gave him work or even a mouthful of food. He could not find clean water. At night, thirsty and dirty, he huddled in doorways to sleep.

Early in the morning of the third day, a kitchen door opened behind him and a voice screeched, "Out of my way, boy, before I kick you into the dog's kennel! Go! Go!" It was the cook in the household of a rich merchant, Mr. Fitzwarren, who lived near Bow Church.

Just then Mr. Fitzwarren came to the door with his young daughter, Alice. He spoke sternly to the cook. "Kick this boy? Do no such thing. He looks half starved. Feed him and give him a decent suit of clothes. He can help you in the kitchen."

Dick was too weak to stand, so the cook jerked him to his feet and led him away. Mr. Fitzwarren's orders had to be obeyed, but the cook did not want a beggar in her kitchen.

She kept Dick busy from daylight to dark doing the dirtiest, hardest jobs. She never lost a chance to beat him about the shoulders with a wooden ladle. At night he could not rest because hordes of rats and mice scampered squeaking in the rafters of his attic room and tormented him by nibbling at his toes.

"How can I get a cat?" Dick asked himself. The Bow Church bell seemed to answer, "I'm sure I don't know." But before long Dick earned a penny for polishing a gentleman's boots.

Dick kept a sharp lookout and
the very next day saw a girl carrying
a tabby cat in her arms.

"Please, miss," Dick said politely, "will
you sell me your cat?"

"Tabby is a very fine mouser," said the
girl. "I would have to get a good price."

"I have only a penny," said Dick, "but I
do need a cat badly." He told the girl about
the rats and mice in his attic.

The girl liked Dick's looks, so she took
pity on him and sold her pet for a penny.

Dick promised to give Tabby a good home.

Dick kept her hidden in his attic room. Secretly he shared his food with her, and in no time at all she killed or chased away the rats and mice. Now Dick slept soundly every night while Tabby kept his feet warm.

Dick made friends with all the servants except the cook, and Alice Fitzwarren liked him more and more. One day she saw the cook whacking Dick's shoulders with a ladle. "Cook," she warned, "if I tell my father what you're doing, you will lose your job."

Not long afterward, Mr. Fitzwarren called all his servants into his study and said, "One of my ships, the *Unicorn*, is sailing tomorrow for foreign parts. Each of you can send something with the ship's captain to trade and make a little money."

All the other servants brought things to be traded. "But I have nothing to send," said Dick.

"Nothing at all?" asked Mr. Fitzwarren.

"Only my cat," Dick answered.

"Then send your cat," said Mr. Fitzwarren; and when he insisted, Dick had to obey.

So Tabby sailed away, leaving Dick Whittington lonely and sad.

Months passed and there was no news from the *Unicorn*.

Back in London, whenever Alice Fitzwarren was out of sight, the cook made mean jokes about Dick because he had sent nothing but a cat to be traded.

On the day of the Lord Mayor's Show, when all of the other servants had
a holiday to see the great parade and join in the singing and dancing, the
cook kept Dick on his hands and knees, scrubbing floors. He was downhearted.

The next day he woke before sunup. I can't stand this another day! he thought. From an open window he heard the deep voice of the great bell of Bow Church. It seemed to say, "Go! Go!"

"I *will* go!" he said to himself. "No more cook!"

Through the empty streets of London he ran until he was four miles beyond the city. There he sat down on a stone to rest and think. Then in the distance he heard Bow Bell ringing, swinging high, swinging low, as if it called,

Turn again, Whittington,
Lord Mayor of London!

Three times he seemed to hear the words.

"Well," said Dick, "if I'm to be Lord Mayor of London, what do I care for the cook?"
He ran all the way back to Mr. Fitzwarren's house and was at work before the cook
had come down to get breakfast ready.

All this time the *Unicorn* had been running into fierce storms and was far off course. At last, by good luck, the ship reached Barbary on the north coast of Africa, where the captain went ashore to trade goods. The king and queen of Barbary were very rich.

The royal couple bought most of the goods on board the *Unicorn* and invited the captain to their palace, where they entertained him in a room hung with silken tapestries. Soft cushions woven with silver and gold were laid out on the floor, where the host and their guests sat cross-legged.

But no sooner had servants brought a feast of fruit and spiced meats than rats and mice swarmed from behind the tapestries. The servants could not chase them away.

"Horrible pests!" cried the king. "What I wouldn't give to be rid of them!"

"Your Majesty," said the captain of the *Unicorn*, "have you no cats in your country?"

"Cats?" asked the king. "What is a cat?"

"I happen to have a cat on board my ship," said the captain. "You will see what she can do."

"Bring her here at once," said the king. "If she can rid my palace of these rats and mice, I will buy her for ten times the price I have paid for all the rest of your goods combined."

When Tabby saw the rats and mice in the king's palace, she jumped from the arms of the captain and went to work. Quick as a wink, the nasty creatures disappeared, tumbling over one another to escape Dick Whittington's cat; and even so, with tooth and claw she killed half of them.

The grateful king and queen gave the captain more than he had ever earned from a cargo. They added a great casket of gold and precious jewels in payment for Tabby.

"You have a bargain," said the captain. "This cat will soon have kittens, and she will teach them to be good mousers."

Richly loaded, the *Unicorn* set sail with a fair wind and calm seas to speed her on her way home to England.

One morning the captain knocked at the door of Mr. Fitzwarren's house. Sailors carried treasure chests heavily loaded with silver and gold into the merchant's study.

"Sir," said the captain, "I have brought you a fortune, and that boy Dick has earned more than you and I together. He is one of the richest men in London!"

"Call him in," said Mr. Fitzwarren. "Tell Mr. Whittington to come to my study."

The servants spread the word through the house. "They said to call Dick 'Mr. Whittington'."

"Nonsense," said the cook. "It must be a mistake."

But it was no mistake. Dick's first thought as "Mr. Whittington" was to share his good luck with Mr. Fitzwarren. "You saved my life when I was starving," Dick said. "My fortune is yours." The merchant would not take a penny. Then Dick offered his treasure to Alice, saying, "You were my first friend." Alice shook her head, smiling. Dick gave generous gifts to the captain and his crew, and to all of Mr. Fitzwarren's servants . . . even the cook.

This was the start of great years for Dick Whittington. He married Alice and became her father's business partner. Three times he was Lord Mayor of London, as the Bow Bell had promised.

But even when he was named Sir Richard Whittington, he did not forget what it was like to be poor and friendless. He gave London its first fountain of clean drinking water. He added a wing to a hospital for homeless young mothers, and he built comfortable shelters for old people.

So when Dick Whittington rode through the streets of London at the head of the
Lord Mayor's Show, all the people cheered and all the church bells were ringing:

Turn again, Whittington,
Lord Mayor of London!

THE BELLS OF LONDON

Oranges and lemons, say the bells of St. Clement's;
When will you pay me? say the bells of Old Bailey;
When I grow rich, say the bells of Shoreditch;
When will that be? say the bells of Stepney;
I'm sure I don't know, says the great bell of Bow.

AUTHOR'S NOTE

Dick Whittington was not only the hero of this famous story, he was also a real boy, born about 1358 in the tiny English town of Pauntley, Gloucestershire. He was still very young when his father died and he went off to London to seek his fortune.

Whether or not a cat helped him, as the story tells, it is true that Dick did make his fortune trading in gold-embroidered silks and velvets, which were worn by the ladies and gentlemen of the royal court. Dick became so rich that he even loaned money to kings. In 1397 King Richard II chose Whittington as Lord Mayor of London. He was elected Lord Mayor in 1406 and again in 1419. He did marry Alice Fitzwarren, but they had no children. When Dick died in 1423, he left his great wealth to help the poor people of London. His history lived on as legend, passed down lovingly from family to family.

THE CHAPBOOKS

For hundreds of years "chapmen" sold the story of Dick Whittington and his cat as they peddled their wares along the roads of England and the English colonies in America. Chapbooks were cheap. They were printed on inexpensive paper and included pictures that often had no connection to the story. Chapbooks were bought by readers of all ages who finally might throw them away or lose them or love them to pieces but never forget them.

In 1763 James Boswell, the biographer of the great Dr. Samuel Johnson, recorded in his *London Journal* how he "went to the old printing-office in Bow-Church-yard where all my old darlings were printed. . . . I bought two dozen of the story-books . . . for he who pleases the children will be remembered with pleasure by the men." The story of Dick Whittington was one of Boswell's "old darlings."

Today we see chapbooks only in a few rare book libraries. The Elizabeth Nesbitt Room Chapbook Collection, Information Sciences Library, University of Pittsburgh, owns a copy of one of the chapbooks Boswell bought so long ago: *The History of Sir Rich[ard] Whittington Thrice Lord-Mayor of London* printed and sold at the Printing-Office in Bow-Church-Yard.

BOW BELLS

In time the "Printing-Office in Bow-Church-Yard" disappeared, and Bow Church itself had to be repaired or rebuilt again and again. During Dick Whittington's time, there was only one bell, but others were added later. Bow Bells have been restored and rehung many times. During World War II, when both church and bells were destroyed in an air raid, the BBC broadcast the sound of Bow Bells as a "recognition signal," bringing hope to the people all over the world who heard them. Now there are twelve bells in the steeple of Bow Church, each bell inscribed with words from the Psalms. The first letter of each of the quotations spells D-W-H-I-T-T-I-N-G-T-O-N.